Young
Squanto

The First Thanksgiving

A Troll First-Start® Biography

by Andrew Woods
illustrated by Chris Powers

Troll Associates

Library of Congress Cataloging-in-Publication Data

Woods, Andrew.
    Young Squanto: the first Thanksgiving / by Andrew Woods;
illustrated by Chris Powers.
        p.   cm.— (A Troll first-start biography)
    ISBN 0-8167-3760-6 (lib. bdg.)   ISBN 0-8167-3761-4 (pbk.)
    1. Squanto—Juvenile literature.   2. Wampanoag Indians—Biography—
Juvenile literature.   3. Pilgrims (New Plymouth Colony)—Juvenile
literature.   4. Thanksgiving Day—Juvenile literature.   I. Powers,
Christine, ill.   II. Title.   III. Series.
E99.W2S647   1996
974.4'004973—dc20   95-10030

Copyright © 1996 by Troll Communications L.L.C.

Published by Troll Associates, an imprint and registered trademark of Troll Communications L.L.C.

Printed in the United States of America.

10   9   8   7   6   5   4   3

Squanto ran through the fields with the other children of the Patuxet tribe. They shouted to chase the birds away from the corn and beans.

The Native Americans worked hard to make
enough food to last through the winter.
They lived near what we now call Plymouth,
Massachusetts.

When Squanto was about 14 years old, he
saw a ship sailing toward shore.

Some of the villagers were afraid of the
strange new people.

But the sailors brought many things to trade,
to show that they wanted to be friends.

7

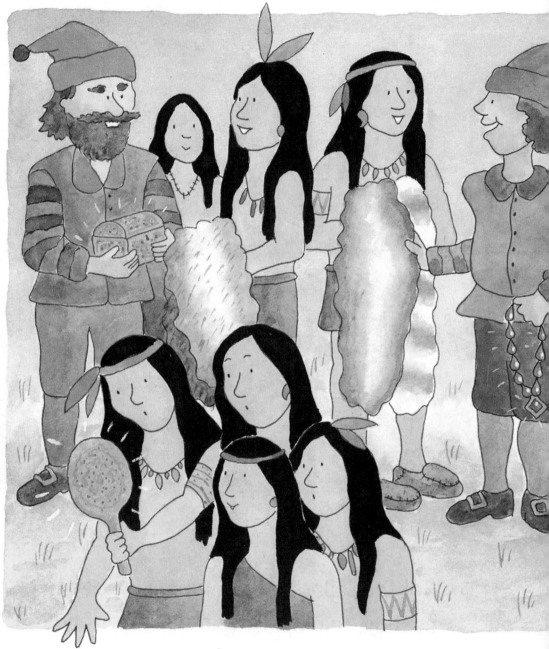

The sailors traded mirrors, bracelets, and
combs for the villagers' warm furs.

Squanto spent much of his time with the
sailors. He even learned to speak English.

One day, the captain asked Squanto to sail with them on their next voyage. Squanto could help the sailors talk with other tribes. Squanto's father allowed him to go.

Squanto was sad to leave his family. But he was very excited to take the trip!

Squanto and his friends began their long
journey. They sailed along the coast,
trading goods with other tribes.

One morning, the ship suddenly changed direction. Squanto was very surprised. He heard the ship was sailing to England!

Squanto was lonely in England, and he missed his family. But he saw many new things. He was very curious and asked lots of questions.

And people were curious about him.
Squanto was not afraid of these people.

Squanto spent 9 years in England. But he always hoped he would see his family again.

One day a sea captain named John Smith
came to see Squanto. He wanted Squanto to
come with him to the New World.

Two ships sailed to the New World.
Squanto sailed with Captain John Smith.

Then one day the captain of the other ship surprised Squanto and captured him. Squanto and many other Indians were taken to Spain and sold as slaves.

Squanto was able to escape to England. After several years, he found his way home and began to look for his family.

Finally Squanto reached the land of his childhood. But there were no crops. There were no people. Everyone had died from a terrible sickness.

Squanto was very sad. He lived alone in
the forest for many months. One day an
Indian named Samoset came to visit him.
He told Squanto there were new people
living where Squanto's home had been.

Squanto went to see these new people.
They were Pilgrims who had come to this
land looking for freedom.

The Pilgrims did not know enough about the land to survive. During the cold winter, many people died.

Squanto decided to help the Pilgrims.
He showed them how to catch fish.

He took the Pilgrims to the hunting grounds he remembered from his childhood.

Squanto helped them plant corn, pumpkins, beans, and other vegetables. He told the children to run through the fields, shouting to scare the birds away, just as he had done as a boy.

When fall came, the Pilgrims were ready to
harvest their crops. They shared the food
with Squanto and their new friends.

The smell of cooked turkeys, wild
cranberries, and warm bread filled the air.
Everybody joined in the feast. They laughed,
sang songs, and played games for days.

They were celebrating the first Thanksgiving.
And the Pilgrims had much to be thankful
for—most of all for their new friend, Squanto.